In My Feelings

Lakeshia Richardson

BookLeaf
Publishing

India | USA | UK

Presentation by *BookLeaf Publishing*

Web: www.bookleafpub.com

E-mail: info@bookleafpub.com

ISBN: 9789360942205

First edition 2024

DEDICATION

I want to dedicate this book to my father James and Sister Latoya, who are no longer here with us on Earth, but always in spirit. I wanted to do something that would make both of you proud of me.

To my mother Adell, who is now and who will always be my biggest supporter. You always have my best interest at heart no matter what and you never lose faith in me.

Finally, to my children Macen and Laila, I just wanted to do something special to make you proud. I love you with all my heart babies.

ACKNOWLEDGEMENT

I want to acknowledge all the people who were involved in my writing journey and who helped me creatively. Those who gave me inspiration, encouragement, and support to see it through. I want to thank everyone who played a part in this collection coming to fruition. Finally, thank you to my family, I love you.

PREFACE

This is a book about being human and knowing that it is ok to feel. Knowing that showing emotion doesn't make you weak or less than others, who hide or conceal their feelings. It is about allowing yourself to be vulnerable and open to expressing oneself through emotion.

Sadness

Sadness is something I often feel, but I try my best to conceal it.

Sometimes it's buried so deep down that I don't know exactly where it is but I feel it inside of me.

Sadness has been a lingering feeling that has always been a part of my existence, but so hard for me to reveal it.

Often I wonder if I will ever be free because it is hard to deal with things you cannot see.

Sadness eats away at you, it is something real, not fake or make-believe.

If you aren't the one who is experiencing the feeling, it can be hard to perceive.

Sadness is a feeling that can take you to some truly dark places so you must be aware.

It's an all-consuming feeling that controls and manipulates you to the point of hiding and refusing to share.

Sadness is real and this warning should be proof, that if not handled properly it can ruin you.

Different

Height isn't my best friend. I'm shorter than most people, but still taller than a few.
Not Weird, Just Different

Skinny I am not. I am thicker than most women, yet slimmer than some.
Not Weird, Just Different

Omniscient no, Einstein I'm not even close.
However, I am knowledgeable about many things.
Not Weird, Just Different

Mozart, no way, never written a symphony. I would say musically inclined because I can carry a melody.
Not Weird, Just Different

I can go on and on with this list as far as the eye can see. I may not be great in your eyes, but I am worthy and that's good enough for me.

I do things outside the norm and some may call it strange, even weird.....

But, I'm not weird, I'm just different!

Numb

What is this lack of feeling, this nothingness inside?

Could the nothing this is currently consuming me be feeling?

How can you say you feel nothing, but somehow you still feel?

Could we refer to this feeling of nothing that we feel as being Numb?

Why do I feel numb? Is there nothing more, nothing left for me to feel?

Ah! There is that word again, "Nothing". Nothing, not one thing, meaning not anything, no single thing.

However, if we use nothing to describe not feeling isn't that contradictory or is it a mystery because we are still technically feeling something?

I prefer to say I am numb. I prefer to say that I am deprived of the power of sensation.

This ultimately brings us back to the first question that was asked in the beginning.

What is the lack of feeling that nothingness inside?

To that my answer is Numb!
Numb is the deprivation of sensation, the lack of
feeling that you feel inside.

Numb!!!!

Hope

We are all human every single one of us.
Being human simply means that we all have hope.

Hope it's merely expecting that something will
happen.
We all hope there's something preferably good that
will happen rather than something bad.

Sometimes being hopeful doesn't always turn out the
way that you want it.
The things that you hope for may not come true, no
matter how hard you hope and wish and pray.

This doesn't mean that you should abandon hope and
give up.
It just means that it might be time to be hopeful for
something else.

There's nothing wrong with being helpful because it
only means that you are human.
I'm staying here remains that you never know what to
expect but you can kind of hope to see you through.

Truth

Truth is the quality or state of being true.
Knowing the truth can sometimes hurt you.

Telling the truth isn't negligent, it's the most honest
thing you can do
because it is based on facts.

However, when emotions get involved, you get
overwhelmed and it changes how you act.

Now there's more to it when the two things are
involved.

The situation becomes complicated and too difficult
to be solved.

Nevertheless, it remains that what is true is still based
on fact and/or reality.

Therefore, it's not the fact that is accepted as truth
that hurts, but the emotion involved that hurts us with
certainty.

Peace

Peace is the ultimate goal, that I have in mind.
I am a worker, who takes action whose always on the grind.

Needing peace to settle my racing mind and ease my weary soul.
Relaxation, becoming less tense, and feeling calm is the goal.

Peace is something I need and crave after a long, long day.
It gives me the ability to let go and watch my troubles fade away.

I am happy and overjoyed when I get the chance to rest.
The sensational feeling of freedom I get from knowing this is going to be the best.

Peace is what I have in mind, that is the ultimate goal.
It's the answer, it's the cure to my restless soul.

Invisible

Sometimes I feel like I fade into the black, the background.
Invisible

I am present, I am here, but nobody can hear me or see me.
Invisible

The time spent amongst others I find myself lost in the crowds.
Invisible

I am amazed at how easily I can slip away and blend into the room.
Invisible

How those around me easily move from conversation to conversation while I dwell in the shadows.
Invisible

I don't want to fade into the black, I want to live on the scene.
Somehow I still slither back into the shadows nowhere to be seen.

Invisible

Insecure

Sometimes this is a small amount of shame in me, but
I don't know why I feel this way.
Maybe I'm Insecure?

No matter how hard I try and even if I succeed. I still
feel like I could have done more.
Maybe I'm Insecure?

I open my mouth and I try to speak up, but I quickly
retreat for fear my words won't be heard.
Maybe I'm Insecure?

Second-guessing myself has become second nature to
me. Self-doubt now rents a room in my head.
Maybe I'm Insecure?

While alone I am average height, but in a room
among the many, I feel minuscule and hard to see.
Maybe I'm Insecure?

Learning and understanding my value has been a hard
task. Believing that I matter and never
underestimating my true worth has been the reward.

Maybe I'm NOT Insecure, Just Growing!

Defiant

I have never been defiant, not even one time.
Never strayed from the rules, or colored outside the
lines

I have always followed directions and made sure to
listen
Never once was I told that I needed to pay attention.

I have never been unruly or ready to fight.
Never fussy or rude, always done what was right.

I have never been the one to cause you to feel shame.
Never made a mess or disgraced your good name.

I have never made you angry or caused emotional
strain.
Never made you cry or left you hurting in pain.

I have never before chosen to speak up, now I'm
labeled defiant.
Never disagreed with you and I now choose not to be
compliant.

I have never turned my back on you, it was you who
turned on me.
Never thought it would come to this, I guess I will let
you be.

I have never been defiant, not even one time.
Never thought I would lose you, but we will be just
fine.

Tears

Tears have meaning to those who shed them.
They are much more than a salty liquid that moistens
the eye.

Tears flow freely for many reasons and it truly
depends on the person.
They are shed during moments when you're happy as
well as when you are sad.

Tears come from thoughts that bring you joy, and
some that bring you misery.
They are clever and you never know when you may
make them, but are on standby even if you need to
fake them.

Tears make you human and you're not weak if you
shed them. Nor are you strong if you decide to hold
them in. Don't be afraid to let them go because they
can also be our friends.

We are all human the proof is in our tears, so be brave
and steadfast because they are here to stay.

Tears are not just a salty liquid that moistens the eye,
they are here to chase your fears away.

Naive

I'm a dreamer who dreams, a believer who believes.
Does that make me Naive?

Fairytales make me happy, and I look forward to
happy endings.
Does that make me Naive?

Smiles can make a bad day good and hugs can chase
the pain away.
Does that make me Naive?

Some people do good deeds and some people even do
bad, but they are all just people.
Does that make me Naive?

It's alright to have dreams that make you believe and
fairytales should have happy endings.

Smiles and hugs are good because you can give them
away freely to whoever is in need.

People will be people despite doing good or bad
deeds.

Being positive makes me optimistic, it does not make
me Naive.

Simple

It could all be simple, you just have to choose not to make it hard.

Given two roads, choose to follow the one that is already paved.

Shortcuts exist for a reason, and it's okay to take a few from time to time.

Understand that a great leader must also learn to follow those they lead.

Uphill battles are better fought on an even surface preferably in a group.

It takes two people to fight or argue, but only one to be smart enough to walk away.

Always remember when one door closes, there is another one you can push open.

Sure the birds in the nest look great, but the one you have caged is always more appealing.

Never forget that a glass half-empty, is the same glass that is half-full so be careful not to spill it.

Finally, loving yourself first gives you the practice
you need to love someone else.

So, don't make life hard, when you can make it
simple.

Lust

Lust will make you do some easy things
It will cause you to act in a way that is unfamiliar to
you.

Lust will give you the confidence you never knew
you had
It will make you adventurous, bold, and full of
spontaneity.

Lust will make you hunger and crave things like
never before
It will make you ravenous and seductive

Lust will make you feel sexy and vulnerable at the
same time
It will cause you to broaden your mindset in new
ways

Lust will give you the extra little push and dare you
to push back
It will make you a dominant bring when you
normally live as a submissive

Lust will make you experience things on a whole new
level
It will make savor each moment of passion delicately

Lust will make you give in to your desires with no
regrets
It will elevate your sensual nature and leave you
begging for more.

Lust is not bad or sinful, instead, it's exciting and
breathtaking. Don't be afraid or ashamed because we
can all use a little lust in our lives.

Silence

To many silence means sadness and to others it
means pain.
To me, silence means peace because it is the only
thing that keeps me sane.

I will take silence however I can get it, whether it be
in small does or long breaks.
I love the relaxing feeling silence gives me and to get
it I will do whatever it takes.

Sometimes silence comes in tiny moments flowing
with absolutely no sound.
These are the times and moments when everything in
life makes sense and seems so profound.

I feel the calm inside me grow, allowing me to think
and finally breathe.
I love the feeling that silence gives me and
sometimes that's all I need.

Kindness

There is a saying that " a little kindness goes a long way", but what does that mean?

Maybe it means smiling because it costs you nothing and you can do it freely.
Give someone in need a hug because it may just brighten up their day.

Why do it, because, a little kindness goes a long way!

Try complimenting a stranger, just because it's something nice you can do.
Lend a helping hand to your neighbor, because it could be you.

Why do it, because, a little kindness goes a long way!

Always humble yourself to the fullest extent and try your best not to boast.
You never know when the time may come when you need help the most.

Why do it, because, a little kindness goes a long way!

No matter how small the task or how great the deed.
There is always going to be somebody who is in need.

Always be polite, and thankful for every moment and
each day.
And remember........

A little kindness goes a long way!

Solitude

The thought of being alone doesn't frighten me,
instead, I welcome it because it excites me.

Being alone means I can think openly and focus on
all the thoughts that occupy space in my mind.
Discover answers to questions that are hard to find.

To me, the state of being alone in the realm of
positivity gives me the freedom to think.

It's a desirable state that allows me to provide myself
optimal security and sufficent company.

i have the chance to breathe and relax from the
madness and chaos that engulfs my everyday life.

The blissful state of being alone makes me happy and
I eagerly await for its occurrence.

Fear

Fear is my biggest enemy always lurking in the shadows.

Fear is the greatest opponent I ever faced that left me shaking uncontrollably.

Fear sometimes has me in a chokehold, I'm afraid to take my next breath because I am scared it may be my last.

Fear looks me dead in the eyes and dares me to make my next move, but I don't even blink.

Fear is preparing me to face all things that have frightened me in the past.

Fear makes me wise and more careful of the next move I make.

Fear has increased my agility and my response to danger when it is nearby.

Fear is making me stronger and I now can stand on my own.

Fear has trained me well and now I feel I can finally conquer it

Fear I am ready to defeat you, I am no longer your
prisoner.
I am taking control and I will be victorious.

Growth

Growth is a part of life and all living things need to grow.

Several types of growing are possible for living things to endure.

A small infant grows into a toddler, who then grows into a child, from there into a teenager, and so on until adulthood.

A human, an animal, and even a plant can all grow in height, width, and volume as well.

However, there are other ways in which growth can be seen.

You can grow in wisdom as well as maturity. You can grow curious, consciously, patiently, and in intelligence too.

So when it comes to growth remember it various ways in which you can grow so be fearless because it's limitless where you can go.

Happy

25

What does it mean to be happy?

Everyone has their way of defining what happiness means.

To me happy means that you are filled with joy.
You carry laughter with you wherever you go.

To me happy means that you shine like the sun.
You share your light with those around you.

To me happy means that you have a cozy feeling deep within.
You want to spread smiles and hugs all around.

To me happy means that you live life to the fullest.
You make the most of every moment you have.

To me happy simply means the joy of just being happy.
You are the only person who can define what happiness means to you.

Altruistic

You feel responsible to always sacrifice
You think you must always pay the price.

The one who holds the door so everyone else can
enter
The one who thinks it's selfish to be front and center.

You always give the most, but always receive less
You are always found cleaning up other people's
mess.

The one who always shows up when others are in
need
The one who never gets thanked for their good deeds.

You never take from anyone, even when you need it
most.
You always remain humble, you never brag or boast.

The one who is always regarded as a trusted friend.
The one who sticks around through thick and thin.

You are the one, everyone neglects to praise for your
endless love.
You are the one, the only one that never gives up no
matter what.
Keep being a shining star because you are
appreciated.

Envy

Envy is a dark, clever little four-letter word.
You must beware of the tricks it has up its sleeve.

Envy will bait you and set you up for failure every
time.
You won't notice the trap because it will be wearing
its friendly mask.

Envy can convince you that your friends are against
you.
You will fall for its lies because it has you under its
spell.

Envy can be dangerous when it feels like you are
slipping away.
You will have to fight hard to break free because its
hooks are buried deep.

Remember to be cautious of those who play the envy
game, because they are only out to destroy you and
ruin your name.